THE BOY WITH HALF A BRAIN

WRITTEN BY:
gibson Huston

Library of Congress Cataloging-in-Publication Data:

Huston, Gibson
    The Boy With Half a Brain

Cover design: Willoughby Lam

Contents

This book is dedicated to the many people who helped me on my journey; unfortunately, some have passed away. I want to honor them here, and you will read about a few of them in the book.

Great Aunt Janie Basile
Lisa Donnelly
Great Grandfather Don Gibbs (Grampsie)
Keeley Green
Patricia Huston (GGma)
Ralph Huston (GGpa)
Great Aunt Sharron Hamilton
Clayton Lewick
Virginia Morris Lewick
Bo March
Lisa Marx
Mac McReynolds
Sirous Nourbaksh
Wyatt Salmons

THE MEMORY THAT CHANGED MY INDEPENDENCE

When I was in a Primary Classroom for students 3-6 years old, I was in Pam Shank's classroom at Raintree. In the late fall and early winter, we were coming inside from a frigid Lawrence, Kansas winter day; I remember I was having trouble with my zipper. When my teacher, Pam, saw I was having trouble, she very calmly walked over, took my hand in hers, and walked me to a table where I spent most of the afternoon. She showed me different one-handed ways to zip my coat. She also showed me one of the Montessori Practical Life zipper frames how to button, snap, and tie. I think that little bit of independence that Pam allowed me to build all those years ago, truly helped make me be the strong, determined, kind, independent person I am today. So, Pam, thank you for just being there. I will forever be in your debt.

Part of the Montessori's method is guiding children to be independent. Children try to figure out things for themselves and to find their ways of accomplishing the task.

Maria Montessori said, "The greatest gifts we can give our children are the roots of responsibility and the wings of independence." When a child is 3 1/2 to 6 years old, little victories are very big milestones in their development. It is even a bigger deal when a child with special needs in a Montessori classroom becomes independent. I have a message for parents: It is essential for your children to become independent in their early developing stages as a student learner. Let your child do daily tasks at the home. Never discount the things your children are capable of.

In the late summer of '17, before my first year of high school, one of my friends from the Raintree community, Ruby Powers, took me on a tour of the Free State High School campus. Also, with us was one of her friends, as she put it, "one of my guy friends." This little bit of kindness meant a lot to me and my whole family. I will always cherish the moment and memory, and it will never leave me or my heart.

A quote from Fred Rogers sums up Ruby's generosity and kindness and the light she shines for others:

All I know to do is to light the candle that has been given to me.

Never pass up an opportunity to help someone, even if it is something small like giving a card to the homeless or going on a walk with your neighbor. There are opportunities all around and they could be just around the corner. It can take you places you never would have imagined. Just like my hero, Mr. Rogers, I would like every-one reading to go back and look at his quote, then close their eyes, take two to three minutes, and think about one or two people who are maybe gone or are still with us who shined a light in your life or gave you a light to keep on shining for others. This is what he asked of an audience when he got one of his awards.

My Grandmother did not know if I was going to make it through my health challenges. She always cherished the happy moments. This message below helped her see hope from a different point of view.

Hope is the thing with feathers that perches in the soul, sings the tunes without the words and never stops at all.

—Emily Dickinson.

Grandparents' hope is all around us. It is in the little things people do. Hope is in the long dark tunnels called a journey with glimmers of light. When you are with a part-icular someone, it gives you that warm and fuzzy feeling called love. You will see why this is true through my unique journey through this book.

INTRODUCTION

I am fortunate to be in a family that founded a Montessori school over 40 years ago. Why? Montessori's method of learning is to create learning communities of mixed ages. Her seminal work was with the working poor of Rome, creating a daycare center and at the Orthophrenic Clinic in Rome working with children with special needs. The famous human developmental theorist Jean Piaget did research in Montessori schools because he found them to be such natural social settings.

When my grandparents started Raintree Montessori School in 1978, they were deeply committed to following not only Montessori's mission, but the exact paradigm she developed: mixed ages, including children with special needs. A school that became my salvation as my life unfolded.

I started thinking about writing this book when I was ten years old. I had a story to tell because at this age, I had gone through so much. Some of the early chapters were written on notebook paper.

I have two challenges: reading and writing. As I got a little older and busier with schoolwork, my reading and writing improved. Still, it wasn't until I was 13 that I began to write more chapters in this book during my independent study time in the Erdkinder (Montessori adolescent program) and on the weekends with my grandmother. I want to thank my teacher Clay Kimmi and our consultant Dr. Tamara Cash for their help.

The first chapters were written when I was younger, the later chapters when I was a little older. Now as I graduate from high school, my writing is more complex, and the way I used to write is different too. In the beginning, I wrote with a pencil on notebook paper, but later I either dictated what I wrote or used a computer.

The purpose of writing all this down is to let you know that there is hope no matter what kind of struggle you have in your life. This book wouldn't have been possible without my friends, teachers, and family. There is nothing more important than having a community that cares about you. I hope reading this book will inspire you.

Gibson at age four... after eating a snow cone at the carnival.

GIBSON'S GAME
Shel Silverstein

I will not play a tug o'war
I'd rather play a HUG o' war
Where everyone hugs
Instead of tugs
Where everyone giggles

And rolls on the rug,
Where everyone kisses
And everyone grins,
And everyone cuddles,
And everyone wins!

THE BOY WITH HALF A BRAIN

A Story of a Hope and Promise

CHAPTER 1

WHO IS GIBSON?

I was born in Lawrence, Kansas on May 4, 2002. My name is Gibson Mac Huston. My parents are Dan and Saasha Huston, and I have a younger sister named Bellamy June Huston.

FAMILY TREE

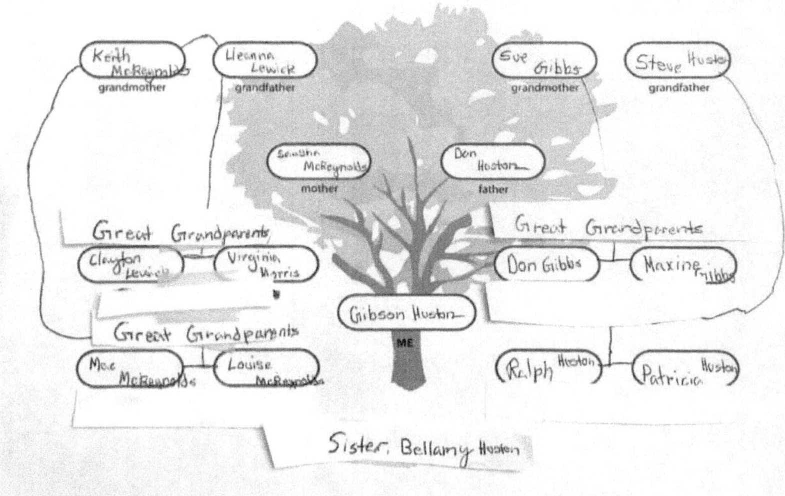

I was named after my great grandfathers, Don Gibbs known as Grampsie and Claud McReynolds, known as Mac Gibbs (Grampsie's name) + son (of Dan and Saasha

Huston) = Gibson. Add the Mac for my middle name, and you get my name: Gibson Mac Huston.

Not only do I have their names, but I have their big hearts and big appetites. They both loved food and I do too. Oh yes, and Mac's love of siestas. Everyday Mac walked home from the bank where he worked at exactly noon. His wife, my Great Grandmother Louise McReynolds, always had lunch ready. She was a great cook. Just as important as eating for Granddad Mac, was sleeping. His nap was always 30 minutes and then back to work.

Grampsie was famous for making jello, really good jello with cherries and pineapple and mandarin oranges. My love of music came from Grampsie and his singing songs with me, such as "Barney Google," "Shave and a Haircut, Six Bits," and "K, K, K, Katie… Beautiful Katie."

Great Granddad Mac.

Great Grampsie Don Gibbs.

CHAPTER 2

LITTLE GIBBY

When I was old enough to attend the toddler program at my grandparents' Montessori school, my first teacher was my aunt Heather Eichhorn.

I am Gibson's aunt. I had the privilege to be included in the birth of Gibby. The idea, honestly, never crossed my mind. I never thought I was someone who would be into that. Birth videos always make me queasy. The birth was long, and, feeling completely useless, I was grateful for the opportunity to "help." I can't think of another word. But help certainly isn't right, as it was all Saasha. Speaking of all Saasha, I confess, I always thought of my younger sister as a soft, sweet, gentle person, not the toughest of women. The birth of Gibson and the trials that have since presented proved that wrong.

When you meet Saasha, you are immediately impressed with her warm smile, and beautiful and sensitive eyes. She is thoughtful and methodical, always reacting with an inner calm. Now I know that on the inside is a strong, stubborn and determined woman.

Back to the birth – it was over two hours of pushing with

no drugs. I won't get into the details, but it was work. In the middle of the pushing, the doctor stopped, exhausted, and said, "I think we need to take a break. Rest, I'll be back." Rest? Are you kidding? I thought. In the middle of pushing? You can't just stop! Finally, he returned, more pushing, maneuvering, and a beautiful, big baby boy was born! Yes, Saasha is strong, one of the strongest I know. And so is Gibby. The birthing process is work for the baby, too

Toddler Years: I remember the excitement of knowing that Gibson would be in my toddler class. How lucky I was to spend long days with my nephew and really get to know him. And what a cutie! As I worked with him and watched him interact with the other children and the materials, it was apparent how similar he was to his mother when she was little — quiet, methodical, thoughtful, and taking everything in.

As a toddler, he was such a gentle, loving child. I knew at home he would fall asleep stroking (or slightly pulling) his mother's hair. Looking back, I recognize that I was giving special attention to him at nap as I made sure that I got to sit next to him and rub his back, but how could I help myself? And yes, before he was able to drift off to sleep, he would reach to find my hair and give it some pulls!

Love, Aunt Heather

One of my classmates was Ruby. For some reason, she

decided to bite me, not once, not two times, but nine times! But there is a good ending to this story which you will read about in Chapter 4: Medicine Affects Behavior. My toddler teachers Heather and Thea said I was left-handed, unusual for someone so young. Later in this book, you will under-stand why I had already developed handedness at such a young age.

My love of food continued. I often took food from friends but in a nice way. Now that I think about it, food and naps were my two favorite things, just like my great-granddads.

Halloween outfits and my Mardi Gras-style parade in downtown Lawrence with my Dad. Organized by Truckstop Honeymoon.

CHAPTER 3

THE BIG SHOW

I can still faintly recall that devastating night when I had my first funny. I remember peacefully sleeping, stroking my mom's hair like I did every night to help me fall asleep. All of a sudden, I got really hot, sweaty, and also very thirsty. I remember asking my mom for some water, but she knew something was wrong... I recall being in the bed and shaking all over. It was like my mind was shutting down and going into that happy place that plays memories from the past, but still in the moment, taking in everything through hearing. The last few things I remember were mom or dad calling nine one one. That's when everything went black. That's the last thing I remember from that night.

Seven months later, it happened again. Dr. Marshall Kelley said we should go to Children's Mercy Hospital in Kansas City and have an EEG test. They put electrodes on my head so that if I had a seizure they could locate where they were coming from in my brain. They wanted me to stay awake most of the night so that I would have one. The doctors wanted to know where the attacks were coming from in my brain. We stayed at a nice hotel to make the best of it. My Granddad has always made the most of a bad situation.

Granddad Keith always made even the scariest experience fun, here getting ready to put shaving cream on me at the hotel after the EEG.

Me sitting in the hospital bed with electrodes on my head.

After that test, they found out that my seizures were coming from one side of my brain. A doctor at Children's

Mercy Hospital in Kansas City told my parents that I may have to undergo a radical surgery called a hemispherectomy to hopefully stop the seizures. They began researching more about my condition. In the meantime, something had to be done to prevent the seizures.

CHAPTER 4

MEDICINE AFFECTS BEHAVIOR

During this challenging time, I was lucky always to have great teachers starting with Heather and Thea, and then Ann Reif and Karla Knudson, and eventually Pam Shanks and Chris Reynolds. One of the things I did was take a lot of medicine which made me behave differently, not like myself at all. In fact, I was tough to deal with sometimes. A mad, or angry feeling would come over me, and I would act out. One day when I was in Ann Reif's classroom, I broke a pitcher, and I had to do many chores at home to earn money to replace the pitcher. Through it all, my teachers never gave up on me.

In this amazing world sometimes we are lucky enough to meet a person that has a charm that shines through no matter what the challenges. Gibson is one of those people.

There was a time in Gibson's life when he was taking medication and it was difficult for him to be himself. The medication made him impulsive and aggressive, which was not typically in Gibson's nature.

Gibson's light continued to shine through. He was loved and supported by his classmates even though they did not understand his struggle. That is what young children do; they adapt and learn from those around them. Our classroom was an environment where Gibson was safe and loved. As Gibson's teacher, I learned bravery, determination, and unconditional love. Friends are friends through the hard struggles and uplifting results that come from seeing those battles fought and won. Gibson was and is an example for all of us

Ann Reif, Primary Teacher

When I was in Pam Shanks' class, I threw the Montessori bells across the room and broke one. Another time I squished a snail, and my friends, who were looking at the snail on the deck with me, were mad that I would do something like that. One time I even spit in the face of a teacher, Jennifer Baker! I now know it was because of the medication I was

Photo of me vacuuming the house to earn money.

taking. I wish I could go back and tell all my friends how sorry I am. And teachers, too, especially Jennifer Baker. You will read more about her and her family and what they did later.

I feel terrible about that because that is not who I am. But I would just get frustrated and mad for no reason. I want to thank all those teachers who put so much effort into helping me. One of the most hard-working teachers at Raintree was Pam Shanks. I moved to Pam Shanks' classroom for my last year in the primary.

Almost from the beginning of my teaching career, Montessori and special education were joint pursuits for me. I often think my life unfolded the way it did so that I would be prepared to be Gibson's teacher.

It was incredibly scary when I found out that Gibson had a seizure disorder. While watching medication fail his little body to the point that his family committed to hemispherectomy surgery, I was convinced it was the saddest thing I would ever see. I was wrong. Before and after his surgery, the medication Gibson took to control seizures changed him. He transformed from a happy, sweet, gentle little boy to one who suffered from fits of rage and aggression. He was still the happy, sweet little boy much of the time, but several times a day, he lost his temper. He would yell, refuse to cooperate, and lash out verbally and physically. Sometimes he even threw things. There were times when I worried about his safety... he was once so angry that he put a hole in the wall. There were times when I worried about the other children in the classroom. I did not want them to be hurt, to be scared, or to copy his behavior. He said things that were so unlike him. For example, his most frequent insult for me when he was angry was, "You are an ugly, old witch." How hard it is to imagine that medication could cause such a transformation, but it did.

It was hard to be his teacher during the worst of those times. I wanted to be fair. I wanted to help him learn. I wanted him to have friends. I wanted him to succeed. I wanted everything for him that I wanted for all of his classmates. I worked harder than I ever had to learn and find new things to help him grow and develop. I tried everything to help him control his outbursts. In that respect, I credit Gibson for allowing me to become a better teacher in many ways.

However, I worked even harder to maintain an image of the real Gibson. No matter how hard the day was I knew it was the medication. Perhaps my biggest worry was that the effects of the medication would be stronger than the love that I had for him, that his friends had for him and that his family had for him. In retrospect, that worry seems silly. The real Gibson was always there.

love, Pam Shanks

I guess people understood I was going through a hard

time because now I had a diagnosis: Hemimegaloencephaly and Hypomelanosis of Ito, two very rare brain disorders. People began to raise money for my surgery. Everyone at Raintree got on board to help.

Raintree parent Jacquie Stineman set up the Gibson Fund. The Saraff family gave a percentage of the profits to the fund from their restaurant, Bambinos. Even Jennifer's husband, Josh Powers, did something really nice for me that I'll never forget to this day. He organized a fundraiser at the Tap Room, where musicians performed.

My daughter tried to eat Gibson.

Ruby was never a biter. Before the "incident," I cannot recall a single instance of her biting anything other than food. Here was my wife, however, telling me that Ruby had not only bitten Gibson, but she had bitten him on his face, and hard enough to draw blood.

This was during Ruby and Gibson's time in the toddler room, where they had been friends basically forever. My wife Jenny has been a teacher at Raintree for the majority of her career, and here was our first child assaulting the grandson of the beloved owners of this beloved institution. Ruby and Gibson's regular interactions were typical toddler stuff – mutual wonder, play, and kissing each other goodbye through the slats in the playground fence at the end of a day.

We apologized up and down to Dan and Saasha and

Lleanna and Keith, and they were – of course – generous in their forgiveness and "pooh-poohing" of what had happened. We tried to divine why Ruby had done what she'd done, but at that age, such answers were difficult to get to.

Fast forward a few years, and Dan and Saasha were in the utterly unknowable-unless-you've-been-there position of facing what my grandfather used to call a "real problem." His actual quote was, "any problem that can be solved with money isn't a real problem," and it was his way of teaching us grand-kids to value what matters: family, friends, your health. Now Dan and Saasha were planning a trip to UCLA so that Gibson could visit a team of specialists to address a potentially life-threatening diagnosis.

The challenge that Gibson faced moved our community greatly, and many people sought to assist the family in any way they could. I collect vinyl records, so I arranged to have a party at a local Lawrence bar to play music and raise some funds to support the Hustons with their travel plans. The night was a success and, I hope, relieved a fraction of the pressure that Dan and Saasha had to think about that particular week.

Fast forward a few more years to now. Gibson Huston hasn't just made it through a challenge that few of us can really comprehend. He has grown into the person, I think, that Ruby saw him as in the toddler room – I think she loved him so much that she got carried away in her toddler expression of love and caring and just tried to take a bite of Gibson's goodness.

And Gibson *is* good; he is the good you look for in the world. Gibson's character is nearly impossible to describe; to say that he's kind is woefully inadequate. To say he's a joy to be around doesn't come close. I wasn't there in the middle of the night when the seizures came, and I wasn't there when Gibson had to learn to walk again. But I have never once seen Gibson mad, unhappy, or anything less than kind and generous to everyone around him.

Again, these things are difficult to put into words, and do justice by in writing. Suffice it to say that Gibson humbles me. I'm proud to know him, and proud that he thinks of me as a friend.

I hope you have the chance to meet him, and more so the privilege to know him.

With love,

Josh

Poster for the benefit Josh organized for me.

Mom and I with Josh Powers at the 8th St. Taproom.

CHAPTER 5

FINDING THE RIGHT HERO

Leaving no stone unturned in finding the best surgeon, my parents went to Johns Hopkins and visited with John Freeman and Diana Pillas, neurologists and hemispherectomy coordinators for Dr. Ben Carson, the famous brain surgeon. They considered Cleveland Clinic, a hospital known for doing the radical operation. They also went to UCLA Medical Center and talked with Dr. Gary Mathern. They decided on him because he had done many hemispherectomies, had a great success rate, and very few kids had to have second or third surgeries. The families and friends at Raintree continued to donate to the Gibson Fund to help us make the trip to California, and former Raintree parents Steve and Joan Craig, who owned a hotel near the hospital, arranged a room for us to stay while we were there.

At Raintree, the parents had t-shirts made for the kids in my class. Orange shirts that said, "Team Gibson." My family wore the shirts, too, so the hospital staff could find them easily in the waiting room if they wanted to talk to them about how the surgery was going. "Find those people with the orange shirts. They're Gibson's people," they would say. Even my friends Emily and Tim Holtzclaw, who lived on the East Coast, were part of the team. They made a snowman and decorated it with an orange scarf and a sign that said, "Team Gibby."

The Lower West Classroom, my class, and my teachers Karla Knudson and Ann Reif dressed in their Team Gibson shirts.

Tim and Emily with Team Gibby snowman.

I'm Gibson's "other Grandpa," the one he didn't see every day at Raintree

More of a weekend Grandpa, later named by his little sister Bellamy "Boompa." Gibson and I liked to sit on the tailgate and listen to rock music LOUD. He sang and danced. He loved listening to me tell stories about his dad when he was a little boy.

Finding out about his condition and surgery was certainly devastating news. Watching him struggle with the medications that "dulled" his usual quick responses made me want to work harder to make him laugh. I felt like his mom had support from her parents and his dad would have his mom there for the surgery. So, I felt like it was my role to try to keep as much "normal" for Gibson as I could. When his first surgery was postponed, we had to pass the time so a trip to Universal Studios did the trick. We could run and laugh and be LOUD! The most difficult time was before his surgery was getting him to take his medicine. It took a lot of different distractions, but eventually, he would take it. At the hotel prior to his surgery one night none of us could get him to, no matter what we tried. So, I bargained with him... if he would take his medications, I would put him on my shoulders and "run up and down the hall," which we did. I would do anything to hear him laugh at that point.

I had to leave before his surgery, but I remember picking them up at the airport when they returned. Of course, it was shocking to see the change. He had a big scar on his head, his smile was lopsided, he couldn't walk. They wheeled him out in a stroller. I got down in front of him closely and in my usual way, very loudly, "Hey Gibby! You're Back!!!!" and it made him smile. Being closer to home I was able to go over to the Kansas City hospital to help him in his rehab. He would be on a machine working his arms so I would get out in front of him and play like he was driving a race car. "Come on buddy. Faster! Faster!" Again, to see his smile was so wonderful. Watching Gib work through that showed courage. He is a true Hero.

Love, Boompa

CHAPTER 6

THE HERO AND SURGERY

When we arrived at the hospital in Los Angeles I had undergone some tests and another EEG to pinpoint the exact location of the seizures in the left hemisphere of my brain. The day before the surgery, my family met with Dr. Mathern to ask him if removing half of a kid's brain would change who they are. Would he still be Gibson? The same Gibson?

Dr. Mathern said he had done lots of these surgeries and said, "Gibson will not change. He will be the same person he is now."

Mimi, my grandmother, said, "That's because Gibson's personality is not in his brain, it is in his heart."

The night before the surgery, our family was eating in the hotel restaurant, and there was a pianist playing music while people ate. At one point, I got up because I wanted the piano player to play a Bob Marley song. She looked through her sheet music and, luckily, she found "One Cup of Coffee Before I Go" and it made me want to dance. Which I did. My parents didn't know I had left the table, but when they heard "One Cup of Coffee..." they knew.

Ali Nourbakhsh, a former Raintree student, one of my mom's high school friends who feels like family and who was a medical researcher, came to stay in the waiting room with my family for the entire 14-hour surgery. Ali could explain what was happening when the doctors came to the waiting room to share how things were going at different times during the long extensive surgery. Our family is forever grateful to Ali and his support during that very difficult time.

After the surgery, my family came to my room. My grandmother was very worried, and she took my hand. I could feel her fingernail and I started rubbing it. And then she knew. Gibson was back! How did she know? Because that was something I did when she and I would rest when I had funnies. Yes, I was back.

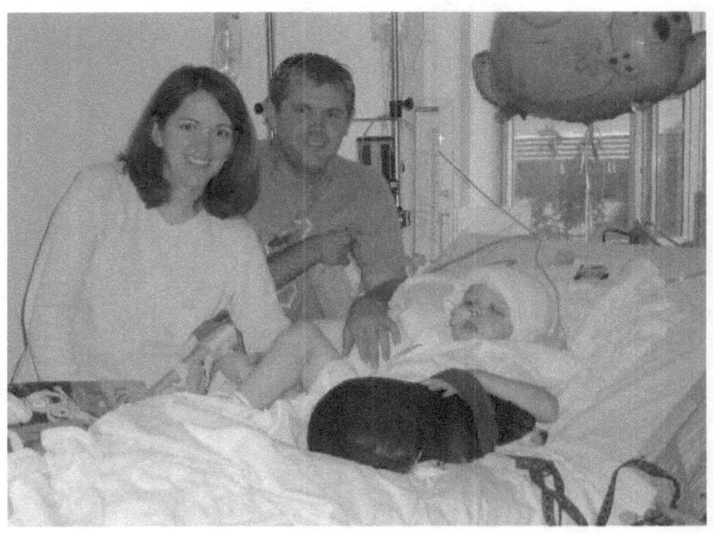

After the surgery with Mom and Dad and my fancy incision.

CHAPTER 7

REST AND REHABILITATION

After we got home, we had to go straight to Children's Mercy Hospital in Kansas City, a great place to rest and get therapy. The nice thing about that hospital was the room service. We could call any time in the day or night and get anything we wanted. It was great.

My Boompa (Grandpa Steve Huston) meeting me at home after my rehab at Children's Mercy.

Our family cheering, happy to finally be home together.

Strengthening my legs on a special trike at Children's Mercy.

CHAPTER 8

FUNNIES STOP FOR A WHILE

A wheelchair helped me get around at Raintree for some time. The kids from my mom's class used to push me in my wheelchair to the car. Raintree was a good place to be because it was set up for kids in wheelchairs with elevators, ramps and pathways.

Mindy Huston was my Occupational Therapist, Carol McBride was my Physical Therapist, and Speech Therapy was with Sharon Haack. Mindy made me do things to strengthen my "righty," the arm that had a mind of its own.

One of the things about getting a hemispherectomy, the removal of one half of the brain, is if the left hemisphere is gone, the right side won't function. If the right side is gone, the left side won't work. In my case, they removed the left side, so I can't see on the right side of both eyes, my righty can be a helping hand, and my right leg doesn't work quite right, so I wear a brace.

I had a hard time talking at first, but I could sing. One of my favorite local bands was Truckstop Honeymoon. Some of my favorite songs were Rockabilly Debutante, Malathion Man, Bad Attitude and Perfect Pair of Sunglasses. I think

Mike and Katie West helped me learn to talk again as I recovered my abilities throughout the years by singing along with them.

Truckstop Honeymoon at Hemi Jam..

CHAPTER 9

FUNNIES RETURN

In August 2009 my sister Bellamy June Huston was born. Now my parents had two children to take care of, and for a while, things were going well.

My sister Bellamy June Huston at age one.

In a Montessori school, kids are grouped into mixed-age communities. I moved into the lower elementary, a group of students 6-9 years old, and my teacher was Laura Shoffner. Unfortunately, I was having funnies again. I had to start taking more medicine, and the medicine made me feel angry again. When I didn't want to go to PT or OT, I would hide in the bathroom with my back against the door to keep it from opening.

The seizures gave me the same feeling you have when you are not telling the truth and your stomach gets achy. You feel lightheaded, that you can't stand, and you are going to fall. You feel sick in your stomach and then throw up. I didn't pass out, but I would feel really tired and stare and wouldn't respond. I felt like I was in my own world. It's hard to explain how you feel. You almost have to experience it yourself.

They wanted to make sure I was okay, but just like before, sometimes the medication made me do things that I wish I wouldn't have done. I had a good friend Sarah Miller who was so kind to me, but when I was angry because of the medicine, I would pull her hair. Really hard. My friends gave me hope that the real me would "come back" one of these days.

Although the seizures were not as bad as they had been, the medicine made me feel weird. My mom and dad talked to Dr. Mathern; he reviewed my tests and determined that I would need another surgery. It would be minor, to remove a small portion of the brain near the brain stem. Our stay was supposed to be short, maybe five days. Mimi went, Granddad and Grandmother, Mom and Dad, and Bellamy, too. Danielle McManus, one of my teachers, sent a remote-control car that I could drive on the ceiling. It could go on the walls, too. It was fantastic. She also sent me lots of Kit Kats, something she sometimes gave to me when I was having a good day in the classroom. Today whenever I see a Kit Kat, I think of Danielle.

Lower Elementary Teacher:

I had the pleasure of being one of Gibson's teachers in his lower elementary years (first to third grade). Gibson had his first surgery a few years before and by the time he was in my class, he was experiencing seizures again, what Pam and he called "funnies." Also, the seizure medicine he took was strong and affected his behavior. Gibson had some helpers in class that year who were amazing. Dana Pauzauskie was the assistant teacher. Danielle McManus-Sykes had just finished her SPED degree and spent the mornings with him, often rewarding his work with a dip into the bottom fridge drawer of mini-Kit Kats. Michael Bradley spent the other half of the day with us, encouraging Gibson's singing and theatrical pursuits. Gibson and I were both about to go through life-altering events, for the better. I was pregnant with my first child and about to become a mother. Dan and Saasha were agonizing over the decision to go back to the surgeon and have another surgery to remove a section of the brain stem that was still causing the seizures. They decided to go ahead with that and headed for surgery in the second semester. We missed Gibson and worried about him (I have often thought that I did not have the mindset of a mother yet). Ultimately it was the right decision and Gibson has been seizure-free ever since that surgery. In Gibson's second and third grade years, he did a lot of work with numbers, beginning reading, and cooking. Sarah Grace Waltz had become the assistant teacher, and Terri Sohl helped for part of third grade. Gibson had returned to being the loving, positive boy he always had been. He put a lot of hard work into strengthening his writing and math skills. He made a beautiful work for the class of "parts of the volcano." My favorite memories of Gibson are in the kitchen. What stands out the most is cooking French bread toast with orange marmalade and cream cheese spread. It was such a warm moment we shared, flipping the toast into the electric skillet, no doubt singing and hugging a bunch while we did it. Also, Gibson sang Elvis Presley songs to the class during pre-sentations time. He wore a bedazzled Elvis costume and had a karaoke session for his birthday party. I cherish the years I had with Gibson and am so happy to have a special connection with such a genuine human being.

I love you. (((Hugs)))
Laura

CHAPTER 10

THE HELPERS

Fred Rogers, the TV star who had a show for many years called "Mister Rogers' Neighborhood," said whenever there is a tragedy, his mother told him to "look for the helpers." I have been surrounded in my journey with helpers. Here is a story from one of many.

During the surgeries, Ali Nourbakhsh's mom and dad, Parivash and Sirous were with my family while the surgery was going on. When I was in bed after the surgery, Ali visited me and made jokes about the monitor, saying Mickey Mouse and Goofy were on the screen.

From far away in California, I learned with so much sadness about my dear childhood friend Saasha's little boy's rare condition. Like everyone who loved her, I was afraid of what the future held for adorable Gibson. And it was difficult to do much for Saasha and her family from thousands of miles away... for this family who had been such an important piece of my childhood and now lifelong friends.

But as fate would have it, Gibson was going to have his major surgery done in UCLA, basically in my backyard. There was no way I was going to let this opportunity to support them slip by. My memory fails me on the details of the day, but I distinctly recall seeing Gibson in his hospital room... a ball of joy despite the challenges he was facing. I remember trying to think of anything at all that I could do to make him laugh, because when he laughed, the room was filled with joy. And I could tell that it made a difference for his dear mother and grandmother, too. The best I could think of was to look at one of the machines in the room that was monitoring something, and the lines looked like Mickey Mouse's ears. So I started imitating Mickey Mouse. I guess it was good, because Gibson was laughing up a storm... and it felt so amazing to connect with this beautiful boy whom I had never spent time with before.

That's the main memory I have—that Gibson, in his vulnerable place as a patient in the hospital, somehow managed to make me feel better, probably more so than the opposite. And I remember telling myself, "That is one special young man."

October of 16, Gibson was giving myself and some friends a tour of the Raintree campus on a golf cart. The little boy who I had feared would never get to live a full life was driving me around and educating me all about the place I grew up in! What an amazing journey. What an amazing young man. I am truly blessed to call Gibson my friend.

Love you so much,

Ali

From Ali's parents, Sirous Nourbaksh and Parivash Nourbaksh:

When we immigrated to US in 1976, one of the first things we needed to do was to put our daughter in school (first grade) and our little son in preschool. That is when we met the McReynolds family for the first time.

Then we didn't know English, didn't know our way around and did not know anybody in Lawrence, but this nice family treated us as a family friend. To this day, this enduring friendship has become even more meaningful as the years go by.

We love Keith and Lleanna, and Heather and Saasha have been like our own nieces. Then we enjoyed seeing the beautiful grandkids. After Gibson's health problems and surgeries, we were afraid that we won't be able to communicate well enough with him to let him know how dear he is to us. But he became an inspiration to our family. Now we are not surprised that he is going to do this project in order to help others. This is what we've been witnessing the McReynolds family doing... helping others!! We love you, Gibson, and are so proud of you and can't wait to see your book.

Love
Sirous & Parivash Nourbaksh

Sirous Nourbaksh was like no other... He was like a Granddad to me. When he visited me after my second surgery and came in my room and sat next to me and held my hand without saying anything, the way he looked into my eyes told me everything is going to be alright. I think Sirous was telling me that "you are going to get through this," and I will be right here waiting for you on the other side. One of my favorite memories of him was when he was pushing my sister in her stroller, and people would say, "What a beautiful granddaughter!" He would say, "Thank you!" That is how I knew he and the Nourbaksh family WERE meant to be in ours. But Sirous Nourbaksh left this wonderful world during the time I was writing this book in early 2018. He died of a heart attack, and I went to the funeral in Georgia. After a few months after the service, I heard Iranian music one day in the car with my dad. I got so emotional listening to the music, but then I remembered Sirous wanting us to be happy and live life to the fullest. Remembering that in the car made me smile. I love you Sirous and the Nourbaksh family.

CHAPTER 11

COMPLICATIONS AND REESE WITHERSPOON

I was about six and a half, almost seven years old. I vaguely remember the uneventful day when I started seizing again for a second time. It was a beautiful start to a fall day when the leaves just started changing in wonderful Lawrence, Kansas. I was watching Cosby with my mom on the couch. I felt very sick. My mom went to get a pot just in case I threw-up. I got up from the couch at the same time my mom came from the kitchen... and in an instant I fell and had a mini seizure. I didn't know if I would make it, and I blacked out.

The next four things I heard and splotches scenes I remember:

I recall my mom on our home phone crying, talking to my dad. I wish could have told her I would be ok, don't worry. The next thing I knew, I heard the front door slam; my dad carrying me to the car, saying you will be ok, don't worry about a thing. I remember and faintly recall the hustle and bustle of the hospital. The last thing I remember were the chopper blades whipping through the wind and the chopper nurse saying, "Put this on!!" And then I blacked out again. When I woke up, my mom was hugging me in a hospital bed in Children's Mercy Hospital in Kansas City because she was so grateful I was alright.

When I reminisce about this memory with family and friends, I would not change anything. My parents would say differently as would others. I think I would not be the same person without what happened to me, and I would not know the wonderful people I met over the years. I also am glad this happened to me because I look at life differently. For example, how you should give everyone a chance no matter what happened in the past. I have one piece of advice for anyone having struggled in life or just having a bad day. The hard struggles in your life and bad days only make you stronger.

You will see why this is true in the stories about my second surgery. Then you will understand why that piece of advice spoke to me when I was life-flighted to Children's Mercy and the second surgery that followed.

Here is a snippet written by my mom from my Caringbridge site when my parents were deciding about a second surgery:

I am humbled and grateful for your kind words today. They have meant so much and, once again, sustained me when I needed it most. Thank you.

We so enjoyed sharing the delicious meal at Raintree in Gibson's classroom. The food and company were just what we needed too. Unfortunately, Gibson had 3 throwing up seizures today and has been pretty wiped out since his last one. He is acting much like he did during the days he was recovering from his EEG in California.

I literally spent the afternoon bombarded by phone calls from doctors and nurses. They must be crossing t's and dotting i's before the holiday weekend. Dr. Mathern called as I was packing Bella up to leave Raintree. Here's what he had to say... The seizures are originating from a 1-centimeter region near the brain stem as he expected. During the disconnection phase of Gibson's last surgery, Dr. Mathern made the separation in front of this tissue, leaving this little bit still attached to the brain stem. In some cases, as in Gibson's, this small bit of tissue began to seize. There is a 50% chance that this second surgery will eliminate these seizures and there's a 50% chance that this surgery will reduce the frequency of these seizures. If Gibson falls into the latter category, it is because the seizures are originating from a deeper part of the brain which cannot be resected surgically. If that is the case, then we have to battle them with medication. We will take the time we need to make this decision and get back to him. He has found that parents have a harder time deciding to send their child in for a second surgery than they do for sending them in for a first. I agree. We are fortunate to have such a gifted surgeon caring for Gibson.

One who diligently follows his patients for years after surgery in hopes of learning more to help the next child.

Dr. Abdelmoity called this afternoon as well. After hearing UCLA's recommendations, he gave me his "2 cents worth." He still feels that the risks of surgery are too great to go forward with it at this point. He pointed out that Gibson is doing well otherwise and doesn't seem to be affected by his seizures. He would like to tweak his medications a little more. He was disappointed that Gibson had come down on the Trileptal. What to try next? I eliminated two medications that Dr. Abdelmoity had in mind. He first suggested an Ativan type medication. It is sustained in the body for a long time having a long half-life. This is out of the question because it is in the same family as Klonopin, a valium-type drug Gibson had an adverse behavioral reaction to four years ago. Dr. Abdelmoity's second choice was Topomax a drug that Gibson was on before surgery. This one clouded up his mind and made it difficult for him to find words that he wanted to say. We finally agreed on a newer drug: Banzel. He will start it on Friday. Because he had such a hard day today, I will up his Trileptal dose back to where it was in hopes of giving him some relief tomorrow. Once the Banzel is on board we hope to wean the Felbatol (another long story... this one is making his reticulate counts borderline) and come down slightly on the Trileptal. I hate to bump up the Trileptal tonight as we have seen a nice improvement in Gibson's ability to keep his behavior in check. Is this related to the Trileptal? I'm not sure. Enough medical details from me... this is making my head spin!

Uh-oh, Bellamy is calling! We are in Topeka tonight to spend time with family. Enjoy time with your loved ones,

Saasha

Even though the surgery went well, I started not to feel well so they moved me to intensive care where they could watch me more closely. My family stayed with me in shifts. Grandmother Mimi, who is a nurse, took the night shift and my other grandmother took the early morning shift. My eyes became very sensitive to light, so they put a mask on me that said, "Closed for business." After a few days, the doctors were really worried about me, and so was my family. One early morning as Mimi and Grandmother were changing shifts, I lifted my head and said, "Watch for the signs." My grandmothers looked at each other and said, "What did he say?"

Mimi said, "I think he said, 'Watch for the signs.'"

A few minutes later, I did it again, and this time, they both heard me and agreed. But why did I say that?

And then the doctors came in to check on me. Half of them were medical students so the doctors explained my surgery and that they were looking for signs of spinal meningitis. One of the head doctors said, "He has spinal meningitis, we saw some symptoms, but we didn't see all the signs." My grandmothers told the doctors what I had said. They were surprised and didn't know what to say.

Yes, I had both bacterial and chemical meningitis, and my hospital stay got longer. Five days turned into five weeks. During that time my family moved to an apartment and continued coming to the hospital in shifts. Mimi returned to Kansas because her sister, my Great Aunt Janie, was dying of cancer.

Janie was special in so many ways, but she passed away during my long hospital stay with meningitis. She came to me in a dream as if to say, "I'm leaving this earth in order for you to complete your journey through life so your loving ways can help others in this world."

My other grandparents stayed. Eventually, I started feeling better and took trips to the cafeteria, where I discovered corndogs, something I had never tried before. Yum.

Reese Witherspoon, a Hollywood actress whose parents were doctors, often visited kids in the hospital. By the way, she is one of my granddad's favorite actresses. One day while Granddad was downstairs pushing my sister Bellamy in the stroller, who should show up but Reese Witherspoon herself?!! Poor Granddad. He was so disappointed and is still disappointed he didn't get to meet her.

The thing about UCLA hospital was its good food. I moved to the apartment with my family and a nurse would visit me and check my PICC line where they could administer antibiotics. They tested my blood, and I would show them how to do it. Granddad freaked out when they took my blood, and I helped them find a good vein.

When I got back to Lawrence, I was a new man. The seizures had stopped. Life was good. The most important thing I learned on this journey was to never give up. There is always shining beautiful days at the end of the long dark tunnel.

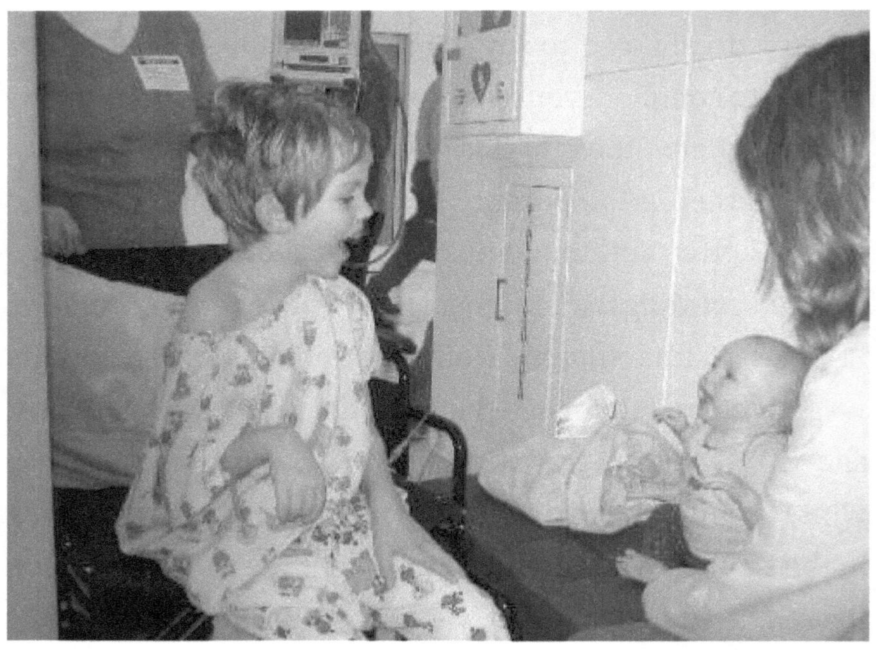

Bellamy and I have a laugh at the hospital for the first time after Surgery.

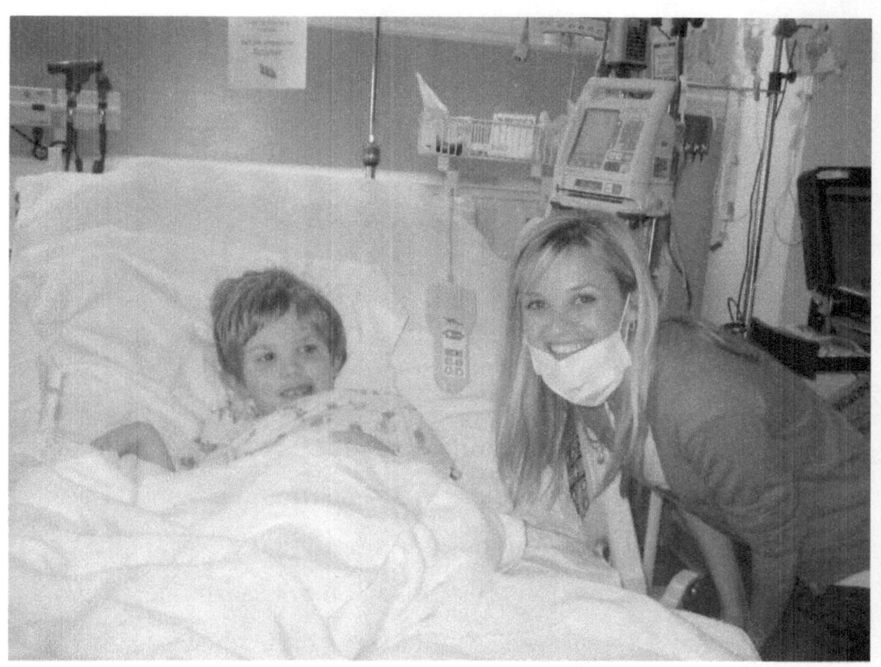

Me with my new friend, Reese Witherspoon.

ature=# CHAPTER 12

GOLDEN HEART

I am Gibson's Grandmother, and he named me "Mimi." I have worked as a nurse all my adult life, though not in pediatrics or neurology. I have been looked to for medical questions. Wow! This one threw me for a loop for sure. I had never heard of Hemimegaloencephaly. When Gibson's mom Saasha called and told me that diagnosis, all I could do was break the word down to "half the brain is large."

When it finally came time for surgery Gibson's parents, Dan and Saasha both were much better informed about the condition and surgery than I knew, I wanted to be there to help them maneuver through the hospital system. I wanted to be there to do what needed to be done so his parents could not think of anything but Gibson and themselves. Things like laundry, groceries, running back to the hotel for what they forgot, etc... I would be the one to stay with him when others were resting which wasn't hard after working as a "night nurse." Those hours with Gibson at night, in the dark, just us, were very special to me. I would sing him "Grampsie" songs and tell him stories about family. And I would just lay my head next to him just like when he would stay the night with me. I know he probably slept through it all with medication. But if he was too awake for a moment, I wanted him to see he wasn't alone. And of course, I wanted to be the one to make sure the staff knew exactly what he wanted and that he would get it. It was very fortunate that I had two cousins and their families that lived in the L.A. area, and they made themselves available for any help we needed... Transportation, housing and recreation. One cousin lived on a beach John and Diane and the other Jim and Connie took us on their boat on the ocean. I learned that in the most difficult times is when you can see the very best in people. And I learned to accept help when offered because I knew it was sincere. Gibson's second surgery was different in that we knew what to expect now, he was older AND we had another one with us... his little sister Bellamy. I felt a different responsibility to help Saasha as much as Gibson as she was still nursing, yet so very stressed with the surgery.

Having watched Gibson, his parents and his sister adjust to living daily with challenges Gibson has lived with and those he has overcome has been amazing. I am so happy Gibson has chosen to write about his life experiences. It has been unique as is Gibson. He could have chosen to be angry or bitter about his challenges. But he did not. He is patient and loving and has only kind and positive words for everything. He is an old soul and I am sure his book will help many others as they face their own unique challenges.

Love, Mimi

When Grampsie died, I was recovering from my second brain surgery. I attended Grampsie's service. I did participate in the service a little bit, but I felt I should have done more for that wonderful special human being and shared how much I loved him.

If I could have spoken at his Celebration of Life, this is what I would have said:

Grampsie, thank you for being in my life. I truly couldn't have gotten through my challenging times without you. You were the reason I kept on fighting on through the harder days, through surgery and recovery. When I was learning to walk and how to stand, and when I wanted to give up, I remembered you were waiting and hoping I would come home again. I needed to be there for you in the years to come. When people tried to give up, you shined a light through the darkness when no other light was found. I remember that hard day like it was yesterday and practicing walking again. I tried to give up, but inside of me I could hear you were telling me, "You can do this." I believed in you, and then I took my first step, and you were right.

A poem I wrote about Grampsie in my junior year of high school for my Creative Writing class and now for all of you around the world

HEART OF GOLD

His face, very warm and friendly and familiar,

A smile still stands out in memory,

The touch of his hands lights up my world
more than my own ever could.

Kinder than his heart of gold,
Lovable as one of the rhythms to his songs,

The way he talked was sincere like the television
neighbor we all know.

You are the kind of person we look for in the world and
strive to become with ourselves and others.

Love, Gibson

CHAPTER 13

MORE HEROES

When I was nine years old, my grandmother played an Elvis song on the radio for me. It made me want to sing and dance. After that, I went to Mimi's house, and she taught me the Elvis shake. Halloween was coming, and at my school, we dress as someone from history or literature. Elvis was from the past, so I dressed as Elvis in a white jumpsuit. The kids thought I was Michael Jackson. They didn't even know who Elvis was. Thanks to my grandmothers, I knew.

The second trip to Graceland 2017 with both grandmothers, sister and mom.

That fall, my parents took me on a special trip to Memphis, Tennessee, where the King started Rock and Roll. On that trip, I got to see Elvis' home, Graceland. What I remember most were the awesome cars, motorcycles, his plane, and his costumes. I had hoped to see Priscilla Presley when I was there, but she wasn't in town.

CHAPTER 14

GIVING BACK

My parents wanted to do something to thank the community for supporting them during my surgeries, so they organized a Hemi Jam where bands and people came together to help the Hemispherectomy Foundation. My dad and I asked if we could advertise on the radio, and the Master of Radio in the Lawrence community was Hank Booth, who worked at the KLWN radio station. He is known as Mr. Radio in my hometown. Jeremy Taylor interviewed us; and Hank did too, and he had a photographer take this photo...

Hank Booth, Jeremy Taylor and I helping to get the word out about the Hemi Jam on the radio.

Because he got the word out, the benefit was a big success. One of my favorite bands, Truckstop Honeymoon, was there. They raised about $8,000 from the benefit.

CHAPTER 15

THE STAR

After my surgery I did some therapeutic horseback riding. During that time, my parents met Ivo Ivanov, who heard about me from a newspaper article all those years ago. Ivo was a journalist from Bulgaria, and he was also a basketball coach for a community team. He asked my dad if I could join his team. Me, a basketball player?

<u>Just the Beginning!</u>

I still vividly remember the day I first met Gibson without really meeting him... Some days – they choose to stay with you. The weather had been unbearable for months, but that particular September morning was simply exquisite. The sweltering summer had finally decided to take a well-deserved breather. No heat, no humidity, mild breeze and a faint promise of a perfect Kansas fall lingering somewhere around the corner of 9th and Mass. I was about halfway done with my coffee at the "Pig" when a story jumped right at me from the pages of the Lawrence Journal-World. The article grabbed me right by the throat and refused to let go. I kept reading about the amazing

Gibby and his famous hugs, the seizures, the diagnosis, the suffering, the excruciating decision, the big unknown, and the looming procedure. I was shaken and mesmerized at the same time! How much strength must 've taken permanent residence in this little boy's body?! How brave and resilient are his incredible parents?! What does the future hold for this wonderful family? I folded the page and took the article with me... in more ways than one.

Completely unable to stop thinking of the overwhelming challenges the Hustons were about to face, I started following Saasha's fantastic "Caring bridge" blog that chronicled in detail the successful hemispherectomy and the long, steep and winding road to recovery.

A few years later, a follow-up story was published. Gibson was doing great. His jovial personality, intellect, sense of humor, love for music, and incomparable spirit remained untouched by the procedure. But there were challenges still, and that fantastic family was wrestling them down – one by one and with that unparalleled Huston resolve that apparently needs to be trademarked. In the photograph, they were together – all four of them now – smiling and happy. Gibson's mom Saasha said something in that article that stuck with me: "...We realized the surgery, not as an end... It was just another beginning."

Are you familiar with the Hoopsters league? In the cradle of basketball that Lawrence is, the Hoopster league is the top youth circuit for the game. The league attracts the best of the best; teams hold tryouts, and competition is fierce. At the time, I was coaching a Hoopsters team called "The Monarchs."

There were talented kids on the team, but for some reason, we were struggling. The chemistry wasn't there, the effort and dedication were lacking at practice, and the kids were played selfishly. Our best defender was Sarah – a sharpshooter and the only girl in the league. I noticed that all too often, the boys weren't getting her the ball when she was open. In other words, the Monarchs had some serious problems, and we started losing games. I knew exactly what we needed to turn everything around. We needed a point guard with a particular set of skills, so I called Dan Huston and asked if Gibson was available. I was willing to beg but didn't have to – Dan not only approved of my recruiting effort but agreed to help with coaching the team.

With Gibby and Dan on board, things changed almost immediately. The practices were very different. Gibson's gregarious personality is one of the most contagious things in the known universe, so very predictably, it energized the entire team. He worked so hard and was so completely consumed by the drills that just by being around him was enough for our players to pick up a lot of his attitude and devotion by osmosis. Gibson is a "unifier" – he unites people... It is such a rare skill but somehow it just comes naturally to him. He instantly befriended all of his teammates, but Sarah was definitely his favorite.

The turnaround was rapid. Our effort and approach changed, the kids were listening to the coaches again and Sarah was nailing jumpers as the boys started passing her the ball. The Monarchs were winning. and it had a lot to do with their new, tough-as-nails floor general – the one I had met all these years ago on a newspaper page that I now kept folded into a small square in my right pocket on game days.

Meanwhile, Gibson improved dramatically his own basketball skills, working tirelessly on his dribbling, passing, and shooting form. He consistently maked mid-range jumpers and free throws and his ball handling was impressive.

Since he had joined the team late, I needed a clearance from the league to put him in an official game. When it finally arrived, we played against the best and tallest team in Lawrence. The Monarchs did their best but, in the end couldn't quite stay with the opponent. Gibby entered the game in the second half and got within shooting range towards the end. We all felt like we were smack in the middle of some Hollywood production: the clock was expiring; the gym was hot and heavy with tension and our team-unifying hero had the ball in his hands eight feet from the basket. Gibson bent his knees, placed the ball firmly on his shooting hand, released it perfectly and...missed. After an offensive rebound, he took another shot... and missed again... and again. It felt like he was running out of steam. There were literally two seconds left when he managed just enough power for one last jumper. That one had destiny on its side. It arched softly in the air and went right through the net with a gentle whisper as the clock expired. Gibby had scored! The Monarchs went crazy and smothered him with hugs at mid-court. For a few blissful seconds a twenty-point loss felt like a victory. There weren't many people at the game – a few parents, friends and relatives of both teams... But I'll tell you what – they were all on their feet applauding and screaming and whoever was there will never forget it – the moment when it became crystal clear – a little boy with a big heart had come all the way back from a long, dark, tumultuous journey to score his first basket – one of many, many triumphs awaiting the great Gibson Huston in the future. Nothing was going to stop this kid!

The game was over. "You have thirty seconds for analysis, and you need to vacate the gym!" said the official. The next game was about to start and they wanted us out. It had been a long season and I didn't want the kids to go home devastated by the loss. I wanted to lift them up... to give them a truly meaningful speech. To remind them what's important in life and what is not. To point out that this was the most amazing and transformative season they've ever had. That we have all learned things far more valuable than basketball. That coming together is not easy and it takes work. That getting rewarded in the very last second is only possible if you overcome enough obstacles. That many years from now they will probably forget this game, the Hoopsters league and even me but will always, always remember Gibson's smile when he scored his first basket. Yes, I wanted to tell them all of these things, but I had thirty seconds. Half a miserable minute. I didn't know what to do. I looked into their teary eyes. Sarah... Rowan... Matthew... Chance... my son, Emil... and I noticed that one of them — only one wasn't crying. Gibson was smiling... he knew... no, he had lived my speech!

And as the precious seconds were ticking away, I suddenly remembered his mother's priceless words from the article and this is what I told them:

"Don't cry, guys. Can't you see: this is not the end. This is just the beginning."

Love, Ivo

Life was good, but I still struggled with reading, especially bigger words, probably because of some of the limitations of my vision. Sometimes it feels like I have to take more time to think through things because there is a detour in my brain. One of the people who helped was Judy Kettle, a former Raintree parent, public school teacher, and a reading specialist. And, also, one of the most patient people I know.

From my reading teacher and neighbor, Judy Kettle:

Being a teacher is a wonderful and rewarding job. You get to meet the most amazing people and have the most extraordinary experiences. Teaching Gibson Huston was a privilege and joy. Each lesson was filled with challenges, hard work, and accomplishment. Accompanying the sessions, Gibson displayed a continued sense of energy, good humor, and optimism. I eagerly looked forward to our time together and undoubtedly learned as much from Gibson as he learned from me.

These are things I taught Gibson:
1. Sight words
2. Phonics
3. Strategies
4. Fluency
5. Developing Comprehension

These are things Gibson taught me:
1. How to see the good in all things
2. How to maintain a positive manner even when things are challenging
3. How to persevere
4. How to enjoy each day
5. How to make the people around you feel appreciated and loved

Reading is very important, but equally so are the qualities that Gibson shares and demonstrates. To know Gibson is to be forever changed for the better.

He now enters a new stage of life as a high school student. He's a young man of many accomplishments and talents. Much to my delight, the circumstances of life have allowed him to become my neighbor in rural Douglas County. I look forward to creating many more connections and memories in our new relationship. In a teaching life filled with exceptional students and moments, Gibson holds a most treasured and special spot in my heart.

With affection and admiration, Judy Kettle

I am honored and touched to have had the opportunity to work with and getting know Gibson over the past eight years. I began working with Gibson on reading in the fall of 2009 during his first year at Raintree elementary. I worked with him for two years. I remember having to have a trash can close by in case he had a seizure and had to throw up. I always felt so bad for him. Our reading lessons were shortened in the beginning and increased after the second surgery. It was so rewarding to see his skills and ability to retain those skills increase as he was eased off his seizure meds. We all had a collective sigh of relief. I was so thrilled for Gibson and the Huston/McReynolds family.

Throughout this whole time that I have known Gibson, he

has always given 100% effort to his work. I will always admire this about him, and his wonderful spirit and genuine care for friends and family.

For the past two years, I have been working with Gibson on cross-stitching once a week. It is always the highlight of my week spending time with this beautiful person. We have snacks and visit about the day, family and basically everything! We are having the time of our lives!!! I feel so blessed to have Gibson as a friend and student.

Love, Anne

CHAPTER 16

STILL GIVING BACK AND LETTING THE GOOD TIMES ROLL

When I went to upper elementary, my teacher was Lisa Ryan. She was a fantastic friend and teacher. Lisa was from Memphis, and when she went back to visit her family, she would bring me something from the Elvis gift shop. That's how my extensive Elvis collection started. It is still growing and rolling.

In sixth grade, I threw a birthday party for my teacher Lisa. I sent invitations with Elvis on them, I decorated the library and the golf cart. I invited old students who had been in Lisa's class. The cake had Elvis on it. And I picked her up in the decorated golf cart with purple and pink streamers. She was surprised.

I dressed in a Elvis' gold lame outfit. And sang five songs: Hound Dog, Suspicious Minds, Burning Love, Now and Then and, of course, Happy Birthday.

Where has the time gone? I remember you before you were born. Of course, I didn't get to really know you until years later.

I remember hearing about all your adventures and worrying about you, but as I learn later when you were in my class, I didn't need to worry.

As a matter of fact, when I look back, I can think of more things than I probably taught you. When you were learning how to read, you taught me how not to give up when things get hard. You taught me that it is ok if I have to do things a little differently from everyone else as long as I learn how to do it.

You taught me that if I keep trying, I will get it. Most importantly, you taught me how to embrace each day no matter what you were facing: headaches, surgery, braces, or your weekly conferences☺. You always faced challenges with a positive attitude and a great sense of humor. You taught me not to let the little things that I face get me down.

Oh, yes, you taught me the healing power of Elvis. I found that if I sing, I feel better, and if I sing Elvis tunes, I cheer up immediately. But the best is listening to you sing Elvis tunes. I will always cherish the memory of my birthday party when you sang Elvis songs to me.

So, Gibson, I am so thankful you are in my life. You have made me a better person, and for that, I am forever grateful.

Love, Lisa Ryan

Another Elvis fan invited me to ride in his classic car in an Elvis parade. His name was Bo March, and he was the

kind of person who did kind things for people. I will always cherish that memory, and it was also the day that I met Bob Lockwood, someone you will read about in the next chapter.

At the Hemi Jam with friends the Redmon brothers, in Elvis's black leather outfit.

At the second Hemi Jam I wore the black leather outfit and danced the night away with friends Bella Stull, David and Will Redmon, Laura Willoughby, Samantha Dennon and Walker Koberlein.

CHAPTER 17

THE HEART THAT SHINED LIKE THE SUN

At the third Hemi Jam, I met Lisa Donnelly. Lisa had been a preschooler at Raintree many years ago, but now she was a singer who lived in California. It was so amazing having her perform at the event. She was very nice, and I even danced several times with her. When it was her time to perform, I was talking to some friends, and all of a sudden, I heard my favorite song of hers and I streaked down the stairs, past my friend Mike Willoughby who said, "Hey Gibson, how are you..."

"Good," I said as I raced by him on my way to the dance floor, taking a spot near the stage. I was the only one dancing at that time except for a little kid. It was a great night.

Lisa Donnelly passed away in 2017. She touched so many lives through her music and in so many other ways. I had the privilege to really get to know this fun, kind and special person. Her songs told a story, and they moved people in more ways than one. I will never forget the memories we made together and shared. I would like to quote a line from a song she wrote about a picture "I got a picture of the day we met. It's a little bit faded but I'll never forget." I also have a picture of the memorable day we met. It is also faded a little bit, but Lisa, I will never forget it. You will always have a very special place in my heart.

THE VOICE OF AN ANGEL

*Her Voice rocked like her tambourine
but yet soft as an angel's tears,*

*Kinder than her heart could hold,
Her generosity shined like the sun.*

*She spoke as sincerely as a person I once knew
I wish I could have told you I will always love
you no matter what happens.*

I am always here for you if you need to lean on me.

Love, Gibson

CHAPTER 18

TEAMWORK MAKES THE DREAM WORK

In addition to the Hemi Jam fundraisers, our family attended many gatherings with other families whose children had Hemis. We also hosted two events at my school Raintree Montessori School. One of the grandfathers of students in our school named, Charlie Crabtree was having a birthday party for himself. He invited a famous Elvis impersonator named Bob Lockwood to sing at his party. When he heard I couldn't come because we were having a Hemi gathering at the school, he surprised us by sending Bob to sing in our school amphitheater. He chose the song "Teddy Bear," and he passed teddy bears to the kids and a special one for me.

*[Previous photo]**Top:** Conference participants, Hemi friends and families. **Right above:** Hemi friends with teddy bear given to the group by Bob. **Right:** Me with Bob Lockwood after I took the Elvis from my mother. **Above:** Bob Lockwood with friends Noah Jones, Ryan Doll and Jayna Doll. And my sister Bellamy picking her nose. Sigh.*

He also gave my mother one of his Elvis scarves during the performance and I took it from her during the show. I still have that scarf displayed in my Elvis shrine at home. Bob Lockwood is one special guy. And so is Charlie Crabtree. Thank you, Charlie.

Years later I went to a concert where my friend Bob Lockwood performed for senior citizens. What a guy.

CHAPTER 19

BEING "DISCOVERED"

In the summer before my sixth-grade year, Monica Jones wrote a grant that the National Institutes of Health funded to study kids who have had hemispherectomies. Called the Magnificent Seven, I was one of seven kids who was chosen to attend Robocamp in Downy, California, at the Rancho Los Amigos. At Robocamp, some of the kids I knew also attended: Hannah, Anna, Logan, Sasha, Jessie, and Josie. My dad went with me, and we stayed in a small apartment called 'The Home" for two weeks. I got to work on a huge loco mat that made me look like a transformer, or big robot and an ankle bot where you put on a shoe that is connected to a computer with a brace. You have to move your ankle back and forth to strengthen your ankle muscles. This is where I first did yoga. We also danced a lot, and they had great food for us. They would order in pizza, tacos and ice cream, and sundaes. It was fantastic.

This is the summer I met George DeMott. His daughter Sasha had had the same surgery. He was a character. Not only was he fun, but he also was a great singer. My dad asked him to sing at the next Hemi Jam... and he did.

George DeMott invited me to sing an Elvis duet with him. Elvis came back...this time in a gold lame outfit. We sang a medley including "Jailhouse Rock" and "Burning Love," to name two. I told my grandmother I was going to be discovered that night. My dad's friend John Naughtin live-streamed the Hemi-Jam around the world, including to friends of George's in Las Vegas. After the Hemi Jam was over, he got a call from his friends who said, "George, the kid in the gold lame outfit. He should come to Vegas and sing with us!" So, I was right; I got "discovered" that night.

Hemi Jam designed by friend Ben Rumback

Getting ready to sing with George at the Hem Jam.

CHAPTER 20

"I'VE BEEN EVERYWHERE!"

In sixth grade, for Halloween I was my grandmother, the principal of my school. She said, "You can't dress as me; you have to dress as someone from history or children's literature."

I said, "You are from history. Raintree history." So, my mom punched up my hair, I put on makeup, lots of it, and wore clothes and earrings just like my grandmother. My costume was so good, one of the teachers, Sarah Grace Waltz, walked by my classroom and said, "Oh, I have to tell Lleanna something. There she is," and came into the classroom to talk to me. When I turned around, she was shocked. "Oh, you're not Lleanna!" Best costume ever.

Later that year, I had another surgery, not brain surgery, but on my arm. It was to loosen the tendons. The incision went all the way up my arm. After all, I'd been through, it was no problem.

In my sixth-grade year, all the sixth-graders got to go to Chicago. We earned money at Coffee Cart, selling breakfast things which we make ourselves at home. I had a great

Coffee Cart partner named Ella Diederich. Sometimes we cooked our stuff together at home, and we competed with two sixth-grade friends, twins John and Carson Green, to earn the most money on the days we worked the cart. We hold the most money raised by students!

The best thing in Chicago was going to the Hard Rock Cafe. It was my birthday, so they turned on an Elvis song, and I shook the night away so much that the pennies fell out of my pocket. The last night we dressed up and went to Ruth's Chris Steakhouse. It was amazing, the food was great, and we all had a great time, too.

My grandmother Lleanna.
Pic with Pam, Grandmother

CHAPTER 21

GRADUATION

I graduated from sixth grade, and at the Recognition Ceremony my grandmother and my cousin Quillen spoke for me. This is what they said:

THE TOP TEN THINGS YOU MAY OR MAY NOT KNOW ABOUT GIBSON:

Number 10: He gives the best hugs in the world.

Number 9: He gets up before dawn on Saturday mornings to help his grandmother do jobs at Raintree & is better at driving the golf cart/Gator than she is.

Number 8: He has an Elvis shrine in his bedroom and more Elvis outfits than anyone we know. But he also likes Bob Marley, Michael Jackson, Johnny Cash, Stevie Wonder and the late, great BB King.

Number 7: He makes breakfast for his sister and himself on the weekends so his parents can sleep in.

Number 6: He is the only Raintree student to host a birthday party for his teacher and serenade her with Elvis songs.

Number 5: Is competitive when it comes to making food for coffee cart with his friend Ella determined to make more money than John and Karson Green.

Number 4: He got a sewing machine for Christmas and made the curtains for his bedroom himself out of Elvis fabric, of course.

Number 3: He wants to be Jim Lewis when he grows up.

Number 2: They visited Graceland and wants to go again hoping to meet Priscilla. We tried to explain that Priscilla doesn't look quite the way she did in the 50s, but he doesn't care.

AND THE NUMBER 1 THING YOU MAY OR MAY NOT KNOW ABOUT GIBSON:

He looks on the bright side of life... in fact he doesn't think the other side even exists.

CHAPTER 22

WONDER

The following summer, I was chosen again for Robocamp. My mom went this time, and for breakfast, we went to a cafeteria and had a breakfast burrito every time. It had egg, sausage, tater tots, and salsa on the side. Yum. I also had hot cocoa. Are you hungry yet?

One of the therapists was a big Elvis fan, and he gave me a lot of Elvis stuff. A huge box, so big we had to buy another suitcase to fly back home on the plane. He told me he had five boxes just as big as this box that he wanted me to have. If I returned to Rancho, he would give me another box. You can imagine what my room looks like: an Elvis-museum.

Before we left California, we went to the Special Olympics ceremony at the L.A. Coliseum. Guess who one of the performers was? Stevie Wonder. A little story about that night: My mom and I took a taxi to the Coliseum. But the taxi driver could not get us there, so we walked three blocks to get there. Behind us I saw all these police officers on motorcycles leading two black motorcades. My mom said it was first lady, Michelle Obama; she is speaking tonight, too.

We had bad seats, but we loved the music, and the speech was amazing.

The school year started, and I joined the Erdkinder, Raintree's adolescent program. One of the first things we got to do was to go on an Odyssey trip to Lake of the Ozarks where we went kayaking down the Niangua River, and hiking to Bridal Cave and exploring a castle in the mountains.

And then, on October 23, 2015, I had another surprise. My mom got tickets to Stevie Wonder in Kansas City without me knowing. It was a well-kept secret, except my grandmother almost spilled the beans, but she didn't. We had the best seats in the house the 16th row, and Stevie performed all our favorite songs, the whole CD of "Songs in the Key of Life" from 8pm to almost midnight!! What a great night!

CHAPTER 23

GRADUATION FROM ERDKINDER

I had a great experience in Raintree's Erdkinder program. We ran our own businesses and planned our own Odyssey trips and spring trips, including budgeting and meal planning. Everyone has a job on the trip.

Every eighth grader was responsible for managing an aspect of the program: Chicken Manager, Finance Manager, Kitchen Manager, Egg Manager, and others. I was the Chicken Manager. After my graduation, the next occupations project will be the building of a greenhouse that the students will manage. I am sorry I won't be there for that project but at least I helped sort the poles for the building before I graduated.

Unlike the sixth-year recognition ceremony, where someone speaks for the student, we speak for ourselves when we graduate from Erdkinder. In closing, I would like to include my speech written the way it was the night I presented it. Why this way? Because my visual field is limited, we made each line shorter, and I used red ink for some passages to help me keep my place. So, if you are a

Hemi kid, you could try this technique if it enables you to give a speech or, for that matter any project as well.

I would like to begin with a quote from one of my favorite TV personalities, Mr. Rogers:

"When I was very young, most of my childhood heroes wore capes and flew through the air. But as I grew, my heroes changed, so that now I can honestly say that anyone who does anything to help a child is a hero to me."

I had an unusual beginning at Raintree. I started my career at three months of age in a crib in my granddad's office.

My first classroom was the toddler class with Heather and Thea. It wasn't long after that I started to have seizures.

The only thing that would stop them was medicine: 14 doses every day. The medicines changed my personality and made me angry and misbehave. My poor primary teachers: Ann, Karla, Pam, and Chris.

Eventually, the medicine didn't work, and I had to have surgery to remove half of my brain when I was four years old.

But tonight is not the time to dwell on the struggles of my life. You can read all about them in my book, "The Boy With Half a Brain," an independent study project I began last year in the Erdkinder. The book will be published at the end of this year.

It is to help other people who have struggles in their lives. The message? Never give up.

Some of my fondest memories I have are being Elvis Presley... and being my grandmother.

But there was a purpose behind my costumes. In 6th grade, Lisa Ryan was my teacher. I wanted to do something nice for her, so I threw her a surprise birthday.

But it wasn't your ordinary

birthday party because Lisa isn't your ordinary teacher. She's your friend and she will always be there for you. Plus, she comes from Memphis, Home of the King. I decorated the library and the golf cart with Elvis's favorite colors: pink and purple streamers and we rocked and rolled away the afternoon. I even got to sing Elvis songs.

Oh, the grandmother part? I dressed as my grandmother for Halloween. The costume was so good that one of the teachers thought I was actually Lleanna and came to the classroom to talk to me. When I turned around, she was shocked.

In the summers I went to Robocamp in Los Angeles as part of a research group studying kids with hemispherectomies.

We were called the Magnificent Seven. This is the summer that I met George DeMott.

Not only is he fun, but he also is a great singer. My dad asked him to sing at the next Hemi Jam, the fundraiser my parents hosted to raise money for kids who have to have the same surgery I did. He said yes.

He invited me to sing two Elvis duets with him: Jailhouse Rock and Burning Love. I told my grandmother I was going to be discovered that night. My dad's friend John Naughton live-streamed the HemiJam around the world. Friends of George's in Las Vegas saw it. After the HemiJam was over, he got a call from one of his friends who said, "George, who was the kid in the gold lame outfit? He should come to Vegas and sing with us!" So, I was right; I got "discovered" that night.

See? Never give up.

In closing... I would like to thank all of the people who made my book possible. And I would also like to thank my

teachers who helped me over
the years, starting with:

    Granddad
    Heather
    Ann and Karla
    Pam and Chris
    Laura and Dana
    Michael Bradley
    Sarah Grace
    Danielle and Terri
    Lisa and Chris
    Judy Kettle
    Jennifer Higgins, Anne
Edwards, and Tamara Cash
    And, of course, my
Erdkinder teachers
    Will, Saasha, and Clay

    And all my classmates who
put up with my ups and downs
over the years.
    I would like to end with a
poem by Patrick Overton:

"When you come to the
edge of all the light you
know And you are about
to step into the darkness,

Faith is knowing one of
two things will happen.
There will be something
solid to stand on
Or you will be taught how
to fly."

My life lesson is to never
give up on yourself or on your
dreams.
Thank you.

CHAPTER 24

THE DREAMER AND THE WONDERFUL WORLD

After graduating from Raintree, I went to Free State High School, a large public high school with over 1500 students. This would be quite a change for me, but someone I had known since I was a toddler helped me out: Ruby Powers. In the summer before the school year started, Ruby took me on a tour of Free State and showed me all my classrooms before my first day. Thank you, Ruby! In 2019 I returned the favor by going with Raintree Erdkinder graduate Kwabena Peasah on his orientation day at Free State.

When I started high school, my love of music grew from artists like Stevie Wonder, Aretha Franklin, the late, but great, Frankie Valli and, of course Johnny Cash. But I will never forget who made me like all the different artists, Elvis Presley. I would like to thank Elvis and the Presley Family for inspiring me and getting me through my path through life struggles.

When I started the second semester of my sophomore year at Free State half day and the other half at Lawrence

Virtual School, I took a Music Appreciation class. When the teacher was doing her PowerPoint, and she was talking about the end-of-year project, she said we could do a music video, PowerPoint, or poem. When I decided what I wanted to do, I said to Ryan Kuhn, my para, "Let's do a PowerPoint," but he said, "Don't you want to do something with Elvis?" and I got to thinking. (That's never good when I think because I come up with big ideas!")

I thought of a 1970s Elvis concert while working on this project. I heard that one of our teacher's cousins had bad cancer, and he was expected to live only one year. Another person, Kwabena's dad, had a massive stroke in September 2018 and was still recovering. And my friend, Noah Jones, who had the same brain surgery that I'd had, was just finishing his sixth brain surgery; I thought why not do an Elvis benefit concert? I used the money I had made converting vinyl records to CDs for my Granddad to buy an Elvis Jumpsuit and a fog machine for the performance.

On May 11th, 2019, I invited friends and family to the concert. We didn't charge for the tickets and had an Elvis Memorabilia Museum, too. Our school chefs, Chris Rieke, Don Zahn, and George Holwick made a buffet of Elvis' favorite foods… such as peanut butter/banana sandwiches. We had donation boxes near the Elvis key chains we made as souvenirs, and that night we raised $6,000, giving each of the three families $2,000.

We couldn't have pulled it off without friends Graham and Davita of Backyard Productions, who helped produce the concert, and my school friend Violet Bredemus who videotaped it. I hope this edition of my book also contains a DVD for you of that particular night. If not, there are some photos on the next page.

With so many people needing help, I have decided to do another concert. This time it will be a Johnny Cash/Elvis Presley event.

I am Gibson's grandmother. No, I am not going to brag about my grandchild. That is not the reason for my contribution to this book. Not at all.

You see I am a list maker, a rush-through-life kind of person. Getting things done, checking them off the list is the goal. Smelling the flowers along the way? What flowers? No time for that. Let's keep moving. And then a grandchild is born with a life-threatening disease that only a radical surgery will fix, and you stop dead in your tracks.

I've told the universe, in the middle of the night as Gibson was being rushed to the hospital, or life-flighted to Children's Mercy in Kansas City, take me. My anger would build when he had seizures at school, and I would take him home to rest. Take me. Don't make this kid suffer. I have had a good life, blessed with a loving family on both ends of my life. Take me.

But the universe said no. And so, deep-seated anger, never

expressed, remained. Anger and sadness as I watched his be-havior change every time he took 14 doses of medicines in a pharmaceutical attempt to keep him from seizing. But they never worked. Instead, they changed his loving personality in-to someone who was angry and frustrated.

After it was determined that seizures were coming from the left side of his brain, we were told there was good news. He could have that hemisphere removed with a good chance the seizures would stop. But what would he lose? His per-sonality, his cognitive abilities, his motor skills? And where do you find a surgeon with the expertise to do this radical sur-gery? Enter Dr. Gary Mathern at UCLA Children's Hospital. Our hero. Gibson's savior.

Fast forward to now. The writing of this book was some-thing Gibson decided to do when he was about ten years old. The little boy who went through so much in his short life had a story to tell, and he wanted others to know there was hope. Never give up, is his motto. Mr. Rogers, his hero.

This kid with a big enough heart for all of us who only sees the flowers along the way (and who pointed them out to his crusty old grandmother) is kind beyond kind.

It has been my pleasure to watch the evolution of this book as Gibson found his voice and expressed what has been felt so deeply in his heart. At some points in the writing, I typed while he dictated, and at other times, he wrote his story on sheets of notebook paper.

A few details I want you to know. We are not wealthy people. The things that Gibson writes about in this book are due to the same universe that wouldn't take me. Planets align-ed, families supported us, wagons circled. How fortuitous that 40 years ago we founded a Montessori school, one devoted to Montessori's original vision: to work with children with special needs. The school we had created for other children became a safe haven for Gibson. The people who have joined us in this work are some of the best of the best, also devoted and passionate about helping others. Many have written about their experiences in the book. Never discount the beauty of this universe, the love people have in their hearts.

The flowers were always there. I see them now, and smell and water them regularly

Love

always,

Grandmother McR.

WHAT IS GIBSON DOING NOW?

My final journey down the hill brought me back to Free State after being online for over a year due to COVID. I was graduating from high school, walking past teachers that I had not seen in almost two years. Two stood out: Nolan Henderson and Melanie Smith. It was nice to see them in person again. I cherish the times with all my teachers and hold them close to my heart forever. I remember giving fist bumps and some hugs. Then I remember seeing the blinding lights of the Free State stadium. It seemed like a blur. I reached the field, and I had a realization: this is it. Later I was sitting, taking in everything as I have done most of my life and cheering for my friends. I had accomplished a lot and seen a lot in my high school career. I remember walking across the stage and hearing both of Grandmothers cheering for me from a distance. I remembered fist-bumping Superintendent Dr. Anthony Lewis and thinking to myself, "Grades can take you far. But it does not matter what kind of grades you get. My mom's priceless advice she gave me on the first day of high school 'Gibson It doesn't matter what grades you get; what matters is that you are learning and challenging yourself.' Because your ideas can take you soaring to new heights, and they take you flying into an amazing future."

After high school I attended Kansas State School for the Blind's Transition Program, which helps with daily living skills, budgeting, and job advocating. All students start in the dorms. Students stay there Monday-Friday. Depending on cooking level, they move students to an apartment by themselves then the cottage with roommates for one to two weeks. The first semester, I went to the apartment and cottage quickly. But the most rewarding part of the whole experience was meeting all these wonderful people from all over Kansas. I made amazing bonds with a few wonderful friends. We became known as the five amigos: Taylor, Rich, Roy, Hashim, and myself. Our friendship blossomed and grew throughout the year. KSSB also had admirable staff that were like family.

Starting with Tim and Lori, they felt like parents, a home away from home, with their unconditional love and support for anything we needed. They gave some guidance and also some humor along the way. Val, she truly helped us grow as people and helped us navigate through things with such an inner calm. Her smile brightens people like a ray of sunshine. I am truly thankful for her. Shelby, our friendship is like notes without a staff, it has no rhyme or reason, it just becomes. Mrs. Sittingdown and Tanya, I will always have a special spot in my heart for them both. You are both truly inspiring people talking with us visiting in the afternoons an into evenings just being ourselves because that's what matters in life. Your inspiring wisdom I will carry through decades to come. Thanks to all the supporting staff who made KSSB possible to nurses, paras, elementary staff, cafeteria staff, and everybody in-between, and of course the administration. I say no matter where we all are, we will be together. "We will forever be together, never part joined together in one heart."

Now that I am two decades old, my life's work has come to me more than me finding it. On May 30th, 2022, I had my first day at Bridge Haven Memory Care in Lawrence as Activity Director. Yes, I plan activities and hang out with residents, play games, talk about old shows like Carol Burnett Show, Bewitched, and Andy Griffith Show telling stories about our lives. Isn't it pretty great? I hope to be here for many years to come. Day by day, my residents feel more and more like family. I can tell you that I will be there for each and every resident through thick and thin. I owe my new career to three things: my music taste, my personality, and my amazing grandparents. I finally found 'hip kids' in the residence I work with, as The Beach Boys would say. In a few decades, if I don't write a continuation of the story of Gibson Mac Huston, I want you all to remember that I was always true to myself and I always listened to my heart. That's how I got here today. I never thought about what people thought of me. It really never crossed my mind. I always did it my way and being myself while I was at it. It doesn't matter how you achieve the goal, what matters is you did it your way. I hope you enjoyed traveling the journey of life with me. I hope you took away something and I hope it eases your life.

IN REMEMBRANCE AND THANK YOU

I spent many years writing this book and during those years, I lost some dear special kind loving friends and family: Sirous Nourbakhsh, Lisa Donnelly, Bo March, my Great Aunt Janie, and great grandmother. Each one of these people had a heart of gold, kind and caring, and willing to take time out of their busy lives to help me. But this is just a fraction of how they touched the lives of those around them. For as long as I live, I will hold them close in my heart and never let them go until the day I die I am forever grateful for their kindness and support.

MEDICAL INFORMATION

HEMIMEGALENCEPHALY AND
CORTICAL DYSPLASIA

Malformations of cortical development (MCD) are increasingly recognized as an important cause of epilepsy and developmental delay. MCD encompasses a wide spectrum of focal and diffuse disorders with various underlying genetic etiologies and clinical manifestations. Disruption at multiple stages of normal cortical development – neuronal proliferation, neuroblast migration, and neuronal organization – lead to characteristic MCD. Focal Cortical Dysplasia (FCD) and Hemimegaloencephaly (HME) are both types of MCD. Still the association of the two is so close that the malformations are often considered as part of their own spectrum. Many see HME as a severe form of cortical dysplasia, though FCD and HME can exhibit a broad range of severity. The dividing line between an FCD diagnosis and HME diagnosis is not always obvious; therefore it can sometimes be difficult to ascertain a definitive diagnosis. To learn more about MCD, please view the presentation, Neuroimaging of Seizures:

Malformations of Cortical Development, in the column to the right.

HEMIMEGALENCEPHALY (HME)

Hemimegaloencephaly, first described by Sims in 1835 and known as unilateral megalencephaly, is relatively rare and characterized by the enlargement and malformation of most or all of a cerebral hemisphere. HME is considered a primary disorder of proliferation wherein the neurons that are unable to form synaptic connections aren't eliminated but accumulated instead. The affected hemisphere may also have focal or diffuse neuronal and glial cell migration defects, with areas of poly-microgyria, pachygyria, and heterotopias. The exact pathogenesis of such a complex malformation is still unknown. Common hypotheses reported in literature are that it occurs due to insults during the second trimester of pregnancy or as early as the 3rd week of gestation, as a genetically programmed developmental disorder related to cellular lineage and establishment of symmetry.

HME is classified into three (3) types. Isolated HME occurs sporadically without hemicorporal hypertrophy or cutaneous or systemic involvement. Syndromic HME occurs in association with neurocutaneous syndromes or developmental disorders (such as Klippel–Trenaunay-Weber Syndrome, Hypomelanosis of Ito, linear sebaceous nevus of Jadassohn, neurofibromatosis, tuberous sclerosis complex, epidermal nevus syndrome, Proteus syndrome) and may occur as hemihypertrophy of all or part of the ipsilateral body. Total HME, the least common, involves enlargement of the same (ipsilateral) half of the brainstem and cerebellum. No chromosomal abnormalities have been associated with isolated HME, and no known inheritance patterns. A gender bias has not been observed in the isolated type, nor has a bias to the left or right hemisphere.

Symptoms often include:

- Abnormally large head and/or asymmetrical head at birth or in early childhood
- Epileptic seizures, especially soon after birth (although these may be delayed until later in infancy or, in more rare cases, into early childhood)
- Developmental delay ranging from mild to severe
- Progressive contralateral hemiplegia – a weakness down one side of the body
- Progressive contralateral hemianopia – blindness in one half of the visual field in both eyes
- Psychomotor difficulties, though not all patients experience these
- The most common with occurrence rate of 90%

Other possible symptoms of the syndromic forms include facial or limb enlargement and/or skin disorders indicative of the particularly associated syndrome or developmental disorder.

Prenatal diagnoses have been reported, though most cases go undiagnosed before delivery. Ultrasound scanning may show asymmetry of the cerebral hemispheres. Ante-natal MR scans in specialist units at twenty to twenty-five weeks may provide additional information. Prenatal screening and genetic advice may be an optional protocol for future pregnancies.

The gross pathology of HME correlates with imaging findings of the affected cerebral hemisphere enlargement. The brain surface may show pachygyria and polymicrogyria. Microscopically, nerve cells are larger and less densely packed than in the normal side of the brain and the number of glial cells is increased. Areas of polymicrogyria, neuronal heterotopia, and pachygyria occur. The white matter may show areas of poor myelination, cystic change, and gliosis. Histologically, there is no difference between FCD and HME. However, HME involves the whole hemisphere macroscopically, whereas FCD is typically more limited.

Treatments may lessen or alleviate seizures and improve the quality of life for HME patients. In most cases, the first line of treatment is AEDs (Anti-Epileptic Drugs). However, current clinical experience indicates that early surgical consideration should be given because of the intractable nature of the seizures associated with HME. Many children undergo and see significant benefits from hemispherectomy surgery. Hemispherectomy is the most effective treatment to control seizures, and it also seems to provide good results on the psychomotor development when performed early. Some neurologists and neurosurgeons are currently of the thought that the earlier the surgery, the better the outcome regarding both seizure control and cognitive impairment. While seizure cessation remains the ultimate goal of this extreme treatment, quality of life improvement scan no longer be ignored as another primary impetus for surgery.

FOCAL CORTICAL DYSPLASIA (FCD)

Focal cortical dysplasia or unilateral cortical dysplasia involves a malformation of part of one cerebral hemisphere, without the enlargement associated with HME. Patients, however, present with similar clinical features and require a similar course of management. FCD is frequently associated with focal epilepsy,; about 76% of patients will have drug-resistant epilepsy. The resulting degree of developmental delay varies from mild to severe.

MRI criteria suggestive of FCD are gyration anomalies, focal thickenings of the cortex, blurring of the grey–white matter junction, and abnormal cortical and subcortical signal intensity. FCD is classified into types and subtypes based on severity and pathology. FCD type 1 and its subtypes are considered mild MCD, while more severe forms are labeled as FCD type 2 and subtypes. Typing based on pathology is as follows: isolated architectural abnormalities (dyslamination) (FCD 1a), additional 'immature neurons' or giant neurons (FCD 1b), additional dysmorphic neurons (FCD 2a) and additional balloon cells (FCD 2b).

Some subtypes are thought to originate in the first trimester of gestation due to abnormal cell proliferation; others are believed to emerge later in the third trimester due to abnormal cortical organization. The different times at which the disorders occur may affect the epileptogenicity of FCD and the outcome after surgery.

HEMISPHERECTOMY FOUNDATION CORTICAL DYSPLASIA FAMILY NETWORK

The Hemi Foundation Cortical Dysplasia Family Network is for families of children have with, or persons with. This cortical dysplasia diagnosis has led to hemispherectomy surgery or consideration and exploration of hemispherectomy as a treatment option for resistant drug-resistant epilepsy due to cortical dysplasia. Because this Network is a Facebook support group of the Hemispherectomy Foundation, members need to have registered or be willing to register with the Hemispherectomy Foundation. The purpose of this Network is to allow Cortical Dysplasia families of the Hemispherectomy Foundation the opportunity to connect for family-to-family support. It's an avenue for those families to share successes and worries, to ask questions, to support families that are newer to the CD journey, and so forth. We hope that you will enjoy this newest diagnosis-specific support avenue. While we understand that we share the hemispherectomy connection with many families, there is often added value in connecting with others that share the same diagnosis that led to this surgery.

www.ingramcontent.com/pod-product-compliance
Lightning Source LLC
Chambersburg PA
CBHW051224160726
47994CB00002B/742